Cracks in the Foundation

by

Steve Backlund

(Author of *Igniting Faith in 40 Days*)

This book is dedicated to:
My wife, Wendy - for being an incredible woman
My parents - for the heritage you have given me
Fred Muster - for being my first spiritual father
Danny Silk - for what you have invested in me

Cracks in the Foundation
by Steve Backlund

A look at over 40 very familiar Bible passages and other sayings that can cause "cracks" in our spiritual foundation if they are misunderstood or misinterpreted.

Verses and phrases in this booklet:
- #1 If it be your will
- #2 All things works together for good
- #3 He . . . sends rain on the just and on the unjust
- #4 It is appointed unto men once to die
- #5 God is in control
- #6 The answer to your prayer will be yes, no or wait
- #7 God is sovereign
- #8 We must be balanced in our Christian walk
- #9 But the prince of the kingdom of Persia withstood me twenty-one days
- #10 It is God who heals the sick, not me
- #11 Every time I minister or move forward in God, Satan attacks me
- #12 Give to him who asks you
- #13 Do good . . . hoping for nothing in return
- #14 Do all speak with tongues?
- #15 A thorn in the flesh was given to me
- #16 I am claiming my healing by faith
- #17 All religions have truth in them
- #18 Will you pray for my healing?
- #19 What about Job?
- #20 The love of money is the root of all kinds of evil
- #21 We will never fully understand the mysterious ways of God
- #22 Spiritual warfare is mainly dealing with the devil
- #23 The Lord gives and the Lord takes away
- #24 God will do it in His time
- #25 The greatest among you will be your servant
- #26 All Christians must go through a personal wilderness or desert experience
- #27 You did not have enough faith to be healed
- #28 We are living in the last days

#	
#29	God won't override someone's free will
#30	All who desire to live godly in Christ Jesus will suffer persecution
#31	The anointing of God sets people free
#32	No man can control the tongue
#33	We don't need to be part of church to be a Christian
#34	It's not about me
#35	Let all things be done decently and in order
#36	God helps those who help themselves
#37	Sincerity & having a good heart are the most important things in the Christian life
#38	People close to God are misunderstood and struggle in relationships with people
#39	And every branch that bears fruit He prunes
#40	God is going to kill you
#41	Partial obedience is not obedience
#42	Calling those things that don't exist as though they did

****

2007 - Steve Backlund (ignitedhope.com)

All rights reserved. This book is protected by the copyright laws of the United States of America. This book may not be copied or reprinted for commercial gain or profit. The use of short quotations or occasional page copying for personal or group study is permitted and encouraged. Unless otherwise identified, Scripture quotations are from the New King James Version. Copyright 1982 by Thomas Nelson, Inc. Used by permission. All rights reserved. All emphasis within Scripture is the author's own. Please note that the author's publishing style capitalizes certain pronouns in Scripture that refer to the Father, Son and Holy Spirit, and may differ from other publisher's styles.

ISBN 1-59872-734-6

Why You Should Read This Book

Steve Backlund is known for his wisdom and practical insights on "how to do life." The students in our ministry school - Bethel School of Supernatural Ministry - love him because he always leaves them encouraged and refreshed in their vision. He has an unusual gift to take the mundane and make it exciting, and to take the familiar and make it new. In his great book, *Cracks in the Foundation*, Steve goes beyond adding life to old thoughts; he successfully inspires the reader to take another look at common ideas that have gone unchallenged for far too long. In doing so, he builds a biblically based foundation of understanding that is very significant. In fact, I believe this foundation is necessary for us to fully embrace the reformation that is at hand. This is a book that I wish every Christian would read.

Bill Johnson
Bethel Church
Redding, CA
Author – *When Heaven Invades Earth*

****

If you enjoy this book, go to ignitedhope.com:

- For CD teaching series that will inspire faith and hope
- For sermon downloads of recent messages by Steve or Wendy
- For information on the Backlund's upcoming speaking itinerary
- To contact Steve or Wendy about speaking to your group
- For many free helps to inspire your life

Read Steve and Wendy Backlund's first book, *Igniting Faith in 40 Days*. It will ignite your hope which in turn will cause your faith to go to the next level.

****

Cover: Linda Lee

Advisors: Dan Hale and Maureen Puddle

Introduction – a Paradigm Shift

The term paradigm shift was originally used to describe a change in basic assumptions within the ruling theory of science. It is also used to describe a major change in a thought pattern or a radical change in personal beliefs or organizations. It is a replacing of a former way of thinking with a radically different way of thinking.

When I read this definition (found in Wikipedia) of paradigm shift, I was struck by the phrase, "a change in basic assumptions." All of us have "basic assumptions" about God, others, the world and ourselves. These core beliefs result from our upbringing, our experiences and from religious teaching. They form a foundation for what we expect and subsequently experience in life. <u>If we have the wrong assumptions</u>, then we have "cracks in our foundation", and we will limit what can be built in us and through us.

This is a book that challenges many of the "basic assumptions" of familiar Bible verses and other common phrases. It is designed to help you think through what you believe. It has the potential to "fill" and repair many "cracks" in our thinking that rob us of potential. You may not agree with everything written, but I believe that you will be motivated to go to a higher level in "nailing down" your own beliefs about the key issues that are raised in "Cracks in the Foundation."

What this book is not:
- It is not a final word on the issues addressed.
- It is not intended to stir up critical attitudes toward those who believe things we don't.
- It is not intended to "puff us up" in pride in having knowledge. Correct theology is meaningless unless it propels us to greater <u>intimacy</u> with God and empowers us to <u>impact</u> the world through love and faith.

What this book is:
- It is to help you think through what you believe.
- It will reveal beliefs that can be misapplied, and therefore limit God and open doors for the enemy.

#1 If the Lord wills

The Context: These words by James are directed to those who are making decisions independently from God. "Come now, you who say, 'Today or tomorrow we will go to such and such a city, spend a year there, buy and sell, and make a profit'; whereas you do not know what will happen tomorrow. For what is your life? It is even a vapor that appears for a little time and then vanishes away. Instead you ought to say, 'If the Lord wills, we shall live and do this or that.' But now you boast in your arrogance. All such boasting is evil'" (James 4:13-16). The apostle says that we do not know the details of tomorrow; and, therefore, we should not make personal plans without a heart that says, "If it be God's will."

The Positive: This verse reminds us to not make decisions without putting God as the foundation of our priorities and decisions. We cannot live as though God does not exist, but we are to look to Him for His purposes to be accomplished in us and through us. Our desire should be to glorify God in all that we do. Personal ambition and impulsiveness are not to be the primary factors that cause us to do what we do.

There will be a crack in our spiritual foundation if we use "if it be Your will" in prayer for things that God has already declared are His will. I John 5:14,15 tells us "Now this is the confidence that we have in Him, that if we ask anything according to His will, He hears us. And if we know that He hears us, whatever we ask, we know that we have the petitions that we have asked of Him." If we have a lack of confidence in our praying, then we need to pursue God's Word (and a revelation of His true nature and goodness) until we can pray according to faith and not doubt.

Concluding Thoughts: God has called us to confidence in prayer by knowing His will about salvation, healing, provision, deliverance, etc. We don't need to pray "if it be thy will" about things clearly outlined in His Word. Yes, we need the Spirit to help us every time we pray, but we cannot doubt God's will in what has already been purchased through Christ's death and resurrection.

#2 All things will work together for good

The Context: "Likewise the Spirit also helps in our weaknesses. For we do not know what we should pray for as we ought, but the Spirit Himself makes intercession for us with groanings which cannot be uttered. Now He who searches the hearts knows what the mind of the Spirit is, because He makes intercession for the saints according to the will of God. <u>And we know that all things work together for good to those</u> who love God, to those who are the called according to His purpose. For whom He foreknew, He also predestined to be conformed to the image of His Son, that He might be the firstborn among many brethren" (Romans 8:26-29).

The Positive: When we turn to God with love for Him, with praying in the Spirit and with commitment to His call on our lives; we are promised that everything in our lives will turn out for good. This includes bad things that have happened to us, or wrong choices we have made. What a glorious promise! It may take a while for a complete turnaround to occur, but God starts the process immediately as we turn our hearts to Him.

There will be a crack in our spiritual foundation if we believe that this verse says, "All things that happen are good." Unfortunately, many believe that Romans 8:28 teaches that. This conclusion results from a misunderstanding of God's sovereignty. If we believe that all happenings are good, we will also subconsciously think that prayer is pointless. We will be hindered in being able to "resist the devil" (James 4:7) because we will never know what to resist (after all, we might be resisting something for our good even if it is sickness, lack or tragedy).

Concluding Thoughts: Romans 8:28 is one of the greatest promises in the whole Bible. We rejoice in it because our God is able to turn messes into something good! That is truly good news! We are careful however not to become passive and just "let life happen to us", thinking that everything that happens will work out for good. That conclusion weakens our hope, and promotes a victim mentality rather than the confidence in prayer as God intends (I John 5:14,15 and Mark 11:24).

#3 He . . . sends rain on the just and on the unjust

The Context: This is a verse in the Sermon on the Mount where Jesus instructs us in attitudes about mistreatment. " . . . do good to those who hate you, and pray for those who spitefully use you and persecute you, that you may be sons of your Father in heaven; for He makes His sun rise on the evil and on the good, <u>and sends rain on the just and on the unjust</u>. For if you love those who love you, what reward have you? Do not even the tax collectors do the same?" (Matthew 5:44-46). As we consider this passage, we recognize that this phrase has often been taken out of context to define rain as negative life circumstances which supposedly happen equally to the believer and non-believer.

The Positive: God's people are called to be thermostats, not thermometers. We should not reflect the hatred or persecution of our environment; but mirror the love, forgiveness and blessing of the Father. We "rain" down God's goodness on those who are seemingly undeserving because God did that for us. Yes, we need boundaries in on-going relationships, but our blessing and prayer for these difficult people will help create an open heaven for them to experience God (e.g. consider Saul's conversion in Acts 9 who was forgiven by Stephen in Acts 7:59-8:1).

There will be a crack in our spiritual foundation if we misinterpret this passage and think the rain (referred to here) is negative circumstances. If we conclude this, we will develop a fatalistic view of life; and we will believe there is no difference in the level of blessing between believer and non-believer. This perspective will create doubt in prayer and faith; and will greatly hinder perseverance in seeing God's promises manifest.

Concluding Thoughts: Both the believer and unbeliever face challenges in this life, but the Christian has access to great protection from the "rain" of Satan's "killing, stealing and destroying" (John 10:10). Jesus became a curse for us so that we could be offered the blessing of Abraham (Galatians 3:13,14). This blessing is received by faith and will increasingly manifest as we continue to abide in Him and His words continue to abide in us (John 15:7).

#4 It is appointed unto men once to die

The Context: "For Christ has not entered the holy places made with hands, which are copies of the true, but into heaven itself, now to appear in the presence of God for us; not that He should offer Himself often, as the high priest enters the Most Holy Place every year with blood of another . . . but now, once at the end of the ages, He has appeared to put away sin by the sacrifice of Himself. And as <u>it is appointed for men to die once</u>, but after this the judgment, so Christ was offered once to bear the sins of many. To those who eagerly wait for Him . . . " (Heb. 9:24-28). This underlined phrase is often used to imply that God has a pre-ordained time for us to die (whether we are young or old, it will just be "our time"). As we carefully look at the context of this, it is clear that the emphasis is that Jesus has taken our judgment. This verse is not a statement concerning the timing of one's death.

The Positive: Death is a reality that we must all face. We all have an appointment with death.

There will be a crack in our spiritual foundation if we conclude that God chooses the time for everyone to die. This thinking would be contrary to the overwhelming scriptural theme that "ong life is a blessing and shortened life is a curse. Believing in a pre-ordained time to die weakens faith's prayer for protection, and it would render obedience and disobedience unimportant in affecting whether life or death is released in us and around us. Also, we are told that "the thief comes to steal, <u>kill</u> and destroy" (John 10:10). Part of our enemy's scheme is to shorten lives. In the gospels Jesus dealt with this by regularly raising people from the dead who had died before they should have.

Concluding Thoughts: We don't know all the factors that may cause a premature death in someone's life, but we need to be careful about concluding that God has chosen a time for everyone to die. When Paul was struggling with whether he should live or "be with the Lord" (die), he said, "<u>What shall I choose?</u>" (Philippians 1:22). We have more to do with our longevity on earth than we might realize. Let's press in and possess the promise of long life for fellow believers, for our descendents and for us.

#5 God is in control

The Context: There is no specific Bible verse where these exact words are stated, but this phrase describes God as the final authority in the universe. It is used to give believers the assurance that Satan's attacks and life's challenges have a limit that is controlled by God (see Job 1 and I Corinthians 10:13), and it speaks of God ultimately fulfilling His purposes on planet earth.

The Positive: I Corinthians 10:13 states that we will not be tempted beyond what we can bear. (This is a great promise of God's control in our lives.) Romans 8:28 also tells us that even the negative things in life can be turned to a positive by God as we respond to His call for us and as we "love God." These are two examples of His positive control in our midst.

There will be a crack in our spiritual foundation if we think "God is in control" means that everything that happens in life is God's will. God gave control of the earth to man in Genesis, but Adam and Eve gave this to Satan in the garden. Jesus then came and took these keys of authority from the devil and said, "All authority has been given to me; therefore, go . . ." (Matthew 28:18-20). Matthew 16:15-19 reveals that the keys of "binding and loosing" have been given to those who walk in the revelation that Jesus is the Christ (the anointed one). We, as the people of God, have been commissioned to control the devil, control the speed of kingdom advancement, and control the level of blessing and protection for our lives and that of our descendents.

Concluding Thoughts: There are great scriptural assurances of God's decisive control for us, but His control can be limited by us. Psalm 78:41 confirms this when it says, "Yes, again and again they tempted God and <u>limited</u> the Holy One of Israel." Also, Mark 7:13 tells us that religious systems can hinder God's influence - " . . . <u>making the word of God of no effect</u> through your tradition which you have handed down." When we hear, "How could God have allowed this to happen", we should consider the better question: "How could we (mainly the church) allow this to happen?" We must be careful to not allow the phrase "God is in control" to make us passive and fatalistic.

#6 The answer to your prayer will be yes, no or wait

The Context: This is not a specific scripture passage, but is a common saying in Christianity.

The Positive: James 4:3 says, "You ask and do not receive, because you ask amiss, that you may spend it on your pleasures." This is an example of when the answer to prayer is no. There are other situations where the answer is delayed because there are spiritual dynamics that must come together for the answer to manifest.

We will have a crack in our spiritual foundation if we do not have confidence that our prayers will be answered. I John 5:14,15 says we are to have confidence of answered prayer because of knowing the will of God. Effective prayer is based largely on God's promises and knowing His nature. "For all the promises of God in Him (Jesus) are Yes, and in Him Amen, to the glory of God through us" (2 Corinthians 1:20). Faith believes we receive the answer at the time of prayer. "Therefore I say to you, whatever things you ask when you pray, believe that you receive them, and you will have them" (Mark 11:24). Our belief that we have it is the key to seeing it. If we think that each of our prayers could have a "no" or "wait" answer, then we will be unable to believe before we see, and we will constantly be passive in prayer (because we will conclude that unchanged circumstances are God's "no" or God's "wait").

Concluding Thoughts: There will be more "no" answers to prayer if we have a lack of knowledge of God's will. The key thing to remember is this: <u>we cannot conclude that the lack of seeing the answer to prayer means that God has said "no" or "wait."</u> To do so would create a huge crack in our faith foundation that would rob us from the experience of knowing that we have things before they have manifested.

#7 *God is sovereign*

The Context: "Oh sovereign Lord" (Exodus 34:23) and other references to God's sovereignty are mentioned many times in the Bible (especially the Old Testament). Sovereign means to have supreme authority or power. God truly is sovereign and is above all others.

The Positive: The Christian exults in God's awesome power. In Christ we have a bottom line assurance that nothing can snatch us away from God's love or from eternal life with Him. The devil cannot touch that! Satan's power is miniscule compared to the supremacy of our God.

There will be a crack in our spiritual foundation if we believe that "God is sovereign" means that He makes everything happen in life (nor can we believe that it means that everything that happens is His will). To illustrate this, consider our salvation. "(God) desires all men to be saved" (I Timothy 2:4). His will is that everyone is saved. Is this "will" happening in every life? No. God's will must be believed, received and contended for. Just as God's will of salvation does not automatically happen, other "wills" are not guaranteed either (i.e. blessings, protection, provision, long life, etc.). These additional parts of our "promised land" are sovereignly available to all, but require a response from us for them to increasingly manifest in our midst. Those who passively sit back and say, "If God wants me to have that, He will give it to me", are going to live far short of God's sovereign best for their lives.

Concluding Thoughts: Many are bitter at God because of a misunderstanding of His sovereignty. The "accuser of the brethren" (Satan) first brought accusation against God (when he was talking to Eve in Genesis 3 in the garden). He has not stopped today. If he can place a seed of doubt in our minds about God's goodness, then there is a danger of major foundational cracks in our lives that will lead to wrong assumptions, wrong conclusions and wrong choices.

#8 *We must be balanced in our Christian walk*

Context: There is no specific verse with this phrase, but we can infer that there is to be balance in our lives because of numerous seeming contradictory commands given to us (i.e. have justice <u>and</u> mercy, be prepared <u>and</u> spontaneous, worship <u>and</u> serve, pray <u>and</u> be productive, be joyful <u>and</u> be serious, be administrative <u>and</u> spirit led, be sensitive to people's feelings <u>and</u> be bold, help the needy <u>but</u> don't enable the slothful, etc.)

Positive: Every situation requires specific wisdom to understand which biblical truth to apply. For example, Paul adapted his behavior to influence people. " . . . I have made myself a servant to all, that I might win the more; <u>and to the Jews I became as a Jew</u>, that I might win Jews; <u>to those who are under the law, as under the law</u>, that I might win those . . ." (I Cor. 9:19-21). Paul was a balanced person who could respond successfully in the best and worst of circumstances (Phil. 4:11-13). We too can respond in whatever manner is needed to help people and to advance the kingdom.

There will be a crack in our spiritual foundation if we believe the balanced Christian life is a mixture of faith and unbelief, passion and cynicism, or victory and defeat. Many believers want to embrace a little of every doctrinal teaching in order to have an acceptable, "balanced" Christianity. Unfortunately, this will lead to a dilution of power (through double mindedness) by trying to combine faith in God's promises with traditional explanations for why there is suffering and unanswered prayer. James speaks of this when he says, "a double-minded man is unstable in all his ways." He is refering to the one who does not believe God will do what He said he would do (James 1:8). To live as a "crack free" Christian, we must be single minded and unbalanced in the belief that God's promises are true and that God is good.

Conclusion: Yes, we need to avoid extremes in many areas of life; but many believers are weak, hopeless and confused because of a fear of being considered fanatical concerning the promises and goodness of God. This comes from a tendency to take a little "truth" from every tradition, and then mixing them together to form a politically correct, but anemic (powerless) Christianity.

#9 *But the prince of the kingdom of Persia withstood me twenty-one days*

Context: "Then he said to me, 'Do not fear, Daniel, for from the first day that you set your heart to understand, and to humble yourself before your God, your words were heard; and I have come because of your words.' But the prince of the kingdom of Persia withstood me twenty-one days; and behold, Michael, one of the chief princes, came to help me, for I had been left alone there with the kings of Persia. Now I have come to make you understand what will happen to your people in the latter days, for the vision refers to many days yet to come" (Daniel 10:12-14).

Positive: This passage helps us understand that there is spiritual warfare involved in prayer and life. The prince of Persia is a high-ranking demon who was hindering the answer to prayer. It is important that we recognize the "spirit realm" of demons (Prince of Persia) and angels (Michael) so that we can make a lasting difference in lives and places.

There will be a spiritual crack in our foundation if we expect demons to withstand us now in the same manner as in the Old Testament. This event in Daniel happened before the cross and resurrection – at which time Jesus "disarmed principalities and powers . . . triumphing over them" (Colossians 2:15). The belief that the devil is the same now as in the Old Testament will actually help create a more difficult spiritual experience for us. New Covenant spiritual warfare is not primarily fighting through the devil's resistance, but it is battling through the "lies" in our mind and heart that stand against the knowledge of the victory that we have in Jesus.

Concluding Thoughts: It is true that the devil can be empowered by agreement with him, but he cannot stand or stay when people (who know their authority) resist him and command him to leave in the name of Jesus. Even though it may take time to see the enemy evicted, it would be wiser to believe James 4:7 ("Submit to God, resist the devil and he will flee from you") than to focus on an Old Testament experience of Daniel.

#10 *It is God who heals the sick, not me*

Context: Christians often say this to encourage others to look to God, and not to people, as their source. The Apostle Paul tore his clothes (Acts 14:14) when people started to say he was a god because of all the miracles that were done through him. He knew the importance of being a "sign" that pointed people to Jesus Christ (and not to himself).

Positive: It is vital that we learn to give God the glory and give Him thanks through Jesus Christ for the great things (including healing) that are done through us. Self-exaltation and pride have been the downfall of many (consider Nebuchadnezzar in Daniel 4 and Herod in Acts 12). Jesus said, "Apart from Me, you can do nothing" (John 15:5). Truly, we need to understand that our connection to God the Father through Jesus Christ is the key for divine healing (and all other kingdom benefits) to flow through us.

There will be a crack in our spiritual foundation if we overemphasize God's role in the healing of others and underemphasize our part in the process. Jesus told His disciples to "heal the sick" (Matthew 10:8). The Apostle John told the lame man, "Look at us" (Acts 3:4). God has delegated his authority to us to "heal the sick." The biblical model for walking in this authority (that is demonstrated in the gospels and in Acts) is not to ask God to heal, but to declare healing over lives. (The continual asking of God to heal reveals a big crack in our theology that will limit what is done through us.) Too often the phrase "it is God who heals, not me" is used as a form of "false humility" that lessens personal responsibility and decreases expectation for healing.

Concluding Thoughts: Each one of us will have to "work out" our own philosophy as we walk down the road of bringing healing to others. In doing so, we must determine to stay out of the "ditches" on both sides of this road: false humility and self-exaltation. Truly, we will want to become a part of a new breed of radical believers that has confidence "in the greater works" that we will do (John 14:12), and who also are ravenously passionate to worship Jesus and give Him "all the glory and praise" for the great things that are done.

#11 *Every time I minister or move forward in God, Satan attacks me*

Context: These words are frequently heard in churches and in prayer meetings. It is the apparent experience of many.

Positive: The devil hates Christians who are seeking to advance the kingdom of God. He is prowling around "like a roaring lion seeking whom he may devour" (I Peter 5:8). He especially wants to devour those who are moving forward in prayer, evangelism, leadership, and in obedience to God. It would be foolish for us to ignore the fact that we "wrestle not against flesh and blood, but against principalities, against powers, against the rulers of the darkness of this age . . . " (Eph 6:12).

There will be a crack in our spiritual foundation if we put more faith in Satan's power to attack us than in God's power to protect us. If we believe that the attacks of Satan (with its negative results) are normal, then our expectation of this will actually attract it to our lives (and will thus reinforce this lie as truth to us). Jesus said, "According to your faith, so be it" (Matthew 9:29). Those who believe they are protected will increasingly experience protection in their lives. Those who believe they will be attacked after moving forward in God (or in ministry) will increasingly have that experience in their lives.

Concluding Thoughts: Sometimes we overuse and overemphasize things like, "If the devil is not causing you problems, then you must not be any threat to him." There is some truth in this statement, but it too often creates a crack of believing that difficulty is the true sign of spirituality. Yes, the devil is looking for those he may devour, but he can only devour when there is agreement with him or fear of him. As people of hope and victory, we are to speak more about God's wonderful protection than we do about Satan's attacks and lies. As we do so, we will see that protection increase.

#12 *Give to him who asks you*

Context: "You have heard that it was said, 'An eye for an eye and a tooth for a tooth.' But I tell you not to resist an evil person. But whoever slaps you on your right cheek, turn the other to him also. If anyone wants to sue you and take away your tunic, let him have your cloak also. And whoever compels you to go one mile, go with him two. <u>Give to him who asks you</u>, and from him who wants to borrow from you do not turn away" (Matthew 5:38-42).

Positive: In the Beatitudes (Matthew 5-7) Jesus "upgrades" the type of attitudes the people of God should have. He focuses on heart issues rather than the Old Covenant's emphasis on outward obedience. In the passage above, Jesus is confronting the spirit of revenge and the tendency to overly protect ourselves from being "ripped off" in life. Both of these attitudes reflect a lack of trust in God providing for us in the future.

There will be a crack in the foundation of our ability to influence many if we consistently let the urgent demands and needs of others dictate our daily priorities. The commands in Matthew 5 must be understood in cooperation with other biblical truths and priorities (i.e. family responsibilities, the Sabbath principle, other commitments that we have already made, contracts we have signed, etc.). Those who try to meet every need around them will end up in debt in finances, in relationships, in health, in spirituality, and potentially in many other ways.

Concluding Thoughts: We all must be willing to give what we have to others, but we cannot let "the emotions of the moment" regularly blind us to what God has told us in the past or from the commitments we have made. For example, paying off our debts or being faithful in tithes to our local church may not seem as important as giving to a homeless person, but it is part of getting our priorities in order (which in the long run will cause us to be able to help multiplied more people).

13 *Do good . . . hoping for nothing in return*

Context: "And if you lend to those from whom you hope to receive back, what credit is that to you? . . . But love your enemies, <u>do good, and lend, hoping for nothing in return</u>; and your reward will be great . . . " (Luke 6:34-35)

Positive: In this passage, Jesus is calling us to a superior way of living. He is rebuking the "I'll do something for you if you do something for me" syndrome. We must look to God to meet our needs, and resist the temptation to expect things back from those we have given something to.

There will be a crack in our spiritual foundation if we do not believe that our giving will cause an increase in what we receive in this life. As we look further in Luke chapter six (verse 38), we read, "Give, and it will be given to you: good measure, pressed down, shaken together, and running over will be put into your bosom. For with the same measure that you use, it will be measured back to you." Besides this verse, there are many other Bible passages that exhort us to give with the expectation that we will receive a blessing in this life from our generosity. "He who sows sparingly will also reap sparingly, and he who sows bountifully will also reap bountifully" (2 Corinthians 9:6); ". . . whatever a man sows, that he will also reap" (Galatians 6:7); and again (Luke 6:37-38) – "Judge not, and you shall not be judged. Condemn not, and you shall not be condemned. Forgive, and you will be forgiven. Give, and it will be given to you . . . " It is clear that we are to anticipate an increase from God when we give.

Concluding Thoughts: It is wrong to give to others with the motive to get something back from them. It is just as wrong to not expect to receive back from God when we have given. Indeed, just as a farmer does in in the natural realm, it is important for us to believe that the law of sowing and reaping is one of the basic spiritual laws that will create an increase for us to be truly blessed and advance the gospel.

#14 *Do all speak with tongues?*

Context: "And God has appointed these in the church: first apostles, second prophets, third teachers, after that miracles, then gifts of healings, helps, administrations, varieties of tongues. Are all apostles? Are all prophets? Are all teachers? Are all workers of miracles? Do all have gifts of healings? Do all speak with tongues? Do all interpret? But earnestly desire the best gifts" (I Corinthians 12:28-31). These verses emphasize the diversity in the body of Christ.

Positive: In this chapter Paul reveals the different roles Christians have in the body of Christ. Individual believers are to find their unique place in His church, and honor others for theirs. With this in mind, there will be those who are more prone to operate in miracles, healing, public messages in tongues and in interpreting messages in tongues.

There will be a crack in our spiritual foundation if we believe that some of the gifts are not for us. This false belief will cause passiveness in seeking breakthroughs in the realm of the miraculous. We must be careful to not use our own experience to create our identity or doctrinal beliefs, but we need to contend for the truths of God's Word. In this particular situation ("do all speak with tongues"), Paul is referring to "public tongues" that would occur in a meeting. He cannot mean that tongues are only for a select few because: 1) we are commanded to earnestly desire spiritual gifts (tongues is one of these – I Cor. 14:1); 2) tongues are a key to building our faith (I Cor. 14:4, Jude 20); and 3) tongues are part of the armor of God (see I Cor. 14:14,15 and Ephesians 6:18).

Concluding Thoughts: Oh what a big weakness this little crack can cause. If we believe God sovereignly gives some people certain gifts (and does not do so for others), then we will live in perpetual limitation concerning our potential and destiny. Our personal experience should not create our beliefs about God or ourselves.

#15 *A thorn in the flesh was given to me*

Context: "And lest I (Paul) should be exalted above measure by the abundance of the revelations, <u>a thorn in the flesh was given to me</u>, a messenger of Satan to buffet me, lest I be exalted above measure. Concerning this thing I pleaded with the Lord three times that it might depart from me. And He said to me, 'My grace is sufficient for you, for My strength is made perfect in weakness'" (2 Corinthians 12:7,8).

Positive: Paul had tremendous revelation, powerful spiritual experiences and great boldness. He was a big threat to the enemy; therefore the devil sent a "messenger" (most likely in the form of persecution from people) to harass him. God's grace though was sufficient for Paul to be an overcomer (even if this "problem" did not immediately leave).

There will be a crack in our spiritual foundation if we believe that this thorn was a "messenger from God" instead of a "messenger from Satan" (as is clearly stated). The "messenger from God" assumption will cause us to not put up a fight against Satan's assignments against us. Even though we don't know the exact nature of Paul's thorn, we do know it was from the devil and scripture teaches us that we must take authority over the devil with persistent and confident resistance (James 4:7).

Concluding Thoughts: Here is a baffling question: why did Paul ask God to remove this demonic thorn instead of dealing with it directly? We don't know the full story here, but we need to be careful in our conclusions. This thorn passage and the story of Job are <u>exceptions</u> to the overall scriptural themes of the power of faith and the power of man's authority over the weapons of Satan. We need to carefully study these passages in cooperation with the message of the whole Bible, and not rely on religious tradition in our interpretations.

#16 *I am claiming my healing by faith*

Context: This phrase is not a specific scripture passage, but it is stated by many Christians when pain and symptoms of sickness are still present in their lives.

Positive: Many Bible verses support the concept of "claiming" that we are who (and what) God says we are, even before it has manifested in our lives and circumstances. Joel 3:10, for example, states, "Let the weak say I am strong." We are to "claim" strength even in the face of manifested weakness. Romans 4:17 gives us further insight, "God, who gives life to the dead and calls those things which do not exist as though they did." Concerning healing, Peter urges us to have a personal identity of health and as "the healed one" when he says "by whose stripes you were healed" (I Peter 2:24).

There will be a crack in our faith foundation if we use the formula of claiming healing without attempting to increase our measure of faith through a deeper revelation of God's love, character and promises. Our faith declaration is an important component of our health, but it needs to be mixed with a strong pursuing of God. Also, if we are in a healing meeting and we verbalize a claim of healing before it has fully manifested, we may actually block further needed ministry from those God has brought to us.

Conclusion: "Naming it and claiming it" was a common phrase in Christianity in the 1980's. It was a truth that catapulted many people to receive the benefits of the cross, but this truth was also abused (because of an overemphasis on spoken faith and an under-emphasis on other important spiritual laws). Wise Christians consistently call themselves healed, but they don't limit their divine health plan to just their confession.

#17 *All religions have truth in them*

Context: This is not a Bible verse, but it is a statement commonly heard.

Positive: God has established spiritual laws that are true, no matter who declares or practices them. Most religions understand the blessing that comes from obeying laws of the spirit such as honesty, generosity, sexually fidelity, self-control, kindness, generosity, tithing, hard work, meditation, covenant keeping, protecting our children, honoring marriage, having wholesome friends, meeting regularly with like minded believers, etc. Religious organizations also generally understand that there is a curse released when these spiritual laws are violated. Therefore, most or all religions have truth in them because they rightly recognize that moral choices dramatically influence the quality of life - both now and in the future.

There will be a crack in our life foundation if we believe that "all roads" lead to heaven and that all religions are a path to God. Common sense should tell us this. (Do all roads lead to San Francisco?) There is a level of blessing on many religions (because of an honoring of spiritual laws), but we must be careful to not let that blessing deceive us into assuming that they lead to the truth. Indeed, truth is a person, not a life philosophy. Jesus said, "I am the way, the truth, and the life; no one comes to the Father except through Me" (John 14:6). Religion is man's attempt to reach God and godliness, while Christianity is a relationship with the Person who is Truth. The difference is night and day.

Conclusion: Because of a narrow interpretation of the Bible, Christians sometimes reject powerful spiritual laws that other religions have discovered. It may surprise some to know that the church can learn from other religions to understand God more fully. This openness though cannot undermine the reality that only Jesus (through his sinless life) was able to enter into the spirit realm to: 1) disarm and defeat demonic forces and give the keys of spiritual authority back to men and women, 2) satisfy God's justice concerning our personal sin, and 3) open a way to a relationship with God for now and for eternity.

#18 *Will you pray for my healing?*

Context: This is a common prayer request. James 5:14-15 supports this. "Is anyone among you sick? Let him call for the elders of the church, and let them pray over him, anointing him with oil in the name of the Lord. And the prayer of faith will save (heal) the sick."

Positive: It is a wonderful thing to be able to pray for people and to have people pray for us. James says that the sick are to call for the elders of the church to "pray the prayer of faith" over them. Those who understand that healing is a "benefit" (Psalms 103:3), and a vital part of our salvation (Isaiah 53:3,4), will truly "pray the prayer of faith" concerning sickness.

There will be a crack in our faith foundation if we think that we are to ask God to heal people. Jesus never asked the Father to heal others, and the apostles didn't either. They prayed in faith by speaking to bodies and declaring healing over lives. They realized that healing was already part of their covenant with God, and they were to "release it" by faith into the situation (and not ask for what had already been given). We will have a crack in our foundation if we are unsure if God wants to heal.

Conclusion: It is good to pray for people to be blessed, to walk in health, and to have personal breakthrough. We must though purpose to grow in "praying the prayer of faith." We will impact lives (and see increased health and miracles) as we believe in our authority as Christians. "Therefore He who supplies the Spirit to you and works miracles among you, does He do it by the works of the law, or by the hearing of faith?" (Galatians 3:5). Lets keep hearing the good news that Jesus has purchased healing, and that we have the glorious privilege of imparting this free gift to everyone we can.

#19 *What about Job?*

Context: "Then the LORD said to Satan, 'Have you considered My servant Job, that there is none like him on the earth . . . ' So Satan answered the LORD and said, 'Does Job fear God for nothing? Have You not made a hedge around him, around his household, and around all that he has on every side? . . . But now, stretch out Your hand and touch all that he has, and he will surely curse You to Your face!' And the LORD said to Satan, 'Behold, all that he has is in your power; only do not lay a hand on his person.' So Satan went out from the presence of the LORD." (Excerpts from Job 1:8-12)

Positive: Job loved God in the midst of great problems and tragedy. He is an example to us of being steadfast in extremely difficult circumstances.

There will be a crack in our spiritual foundation if we conclude that God allows Satan to test our Christian love and commitment through destructive loss of property, death of family members and physical affliction. If we believe this (even to a small degree), we will live in doubt concerning God's will about protection, long life, physical health and many other things. The devil (the thief) is seeking "to kill, steal and destroy" things in our lives. We are called to resist the devil to the point where he flees from us (James 4:7). If we think that God has indirectly sent him to us to test our lives, then we will have little power or faith to persevere in our resistance of him (because we will think we might be resisting God).

Conclusion: Job said, "What I greatly feared has come upon me" (Job 3:25). His fear gave Satan a legal access to "kill, steal, and destroy" from him. God "allowed" this attack only in the sense that He has established spiritual laws (such as the laws of fear and faith) that bring an outcome into our lives. Job's situation was not a random, sovereign attack; but it manifested because of a violation of a spiritual law. We will be on a "slippery slope" if we subconsciously believe that God might sovereignly dismantle our lives to test us.

#20 *The love of money is the root of all kinds of evil*

Context: "But those who desire to be rich fall into temptation and a snare, and into many foolish and harmful lusts which drown men in destruction and perdition. <u>For the love of money is a root of all kinds of evil</u>, for which some have strayed from the faith in their greediness, and pierced themselves through with many sorrows" (I Timothy 6:9-10).

Positive: Financial considerations are important in decision-making, but we must submit them to spiritual and family priorities or else we are going to have trouble. When making decisions, our primary question needs to be "How will this decision affect my spiritual life and family life?" When money becomes our greatest love, then we will compromise spiritual laws (i.e. honesty, honor of people, family commitments, generosity, seeking God's kingdom first, etc.), and we will reap a negative harvest as a result. The "love of money" is indeed a "root of all kinds of evil" for many.

There will be a crack in our spiritual foundation if we do not expect and contend for increased financial wealth as we move forward in God. Jesus commanded us in Matthew 28:18-20 to "go" and transform the world in His name. There is no way we can do this without prosperity. It takes a lot of money to evangelize and disciple the world. We cannot just take care of our own needs, but we should tenaciously go after God's principles of financial increase to impact the world. This indeed will help us be obedient to the Great Commission of Matthew 28.

Conclusion: We must resist the temptation of fearing increased wealth in our lives. It is true that many are ruined by "the love of money", and it is true that we must constantly guard our soul from its destructive influence; but we cannot go to the other extreme of believing that poverty is true spirituality. As we grow in Christ, we should expect "an abundance for every good work" to be our testimony (2 Corinthians 9:8-12). This abundance (rightly used) will cause many to be in heaven, and they will be glad that we pressed in for God's abounding provision to flow through us.

#21 *We will never fully understand the mysterious ways of God*

Context: This phrase is not in the Bible, but it can be inferred from Bible passages such as Isaiah 55:8,9. "'For My thoughts are not your thoughts, nor are your ways My ways,' says the LORD. 'For as the heavens are higher than the earth, so are My ways higher than your ways, and My thoughts than your thoughts.'"

Positive: It is vital that we as Christians learn to live with mystery and not think we have to have an explanation for everything in life. When difficult and mysterious things happen, we should be comfortable in saying, "I don't know why this happened, but one thing that I do know is this: any God who would send His only Son to die for us is good, very good." Also, it is vital to know that the unresolved, mysterious happenings of life have a "door" attached to them that will lead to greater revelation of God and His goodness. This door can be passed through as we overcome bitterness and the temptation to create our doctrine (God concept) from our negative experiences.

There will be a crack in our spiritual foundation if we allow the "God is mysterious" thinking to lead us to a place where we subconsciously conclude that everything that happens is His will. "After all," we might say, "God may have a reason for why He wants this person left sick, or in lack, or to have that accident, or to experience that abuse, or to die early in life." That conclusion will leave a crack in our faith, and we will not be able to pray in faith and confidence because we might be coming against a mysterious thing that God is doing.

Conclusion: We realize that there are often other factors to be addressed besides prayer and faith to see God's will manifest, but we need to be cautious to not use the "God is mysterious" theology as an excuse for why we are not resisting Satan's "stealing, killing and destroying" from lives. Do our beliefs lead us to fatalism, hopelessness and passiveness; or do they lead us to a burning and sacrificial realization that we can change the world and history in the name of Jesus? How we interpret the mysteriousness of God will be a huge factor in what direction we take.

#22 Spiritual warfare is mainly dealing with the devil

Context: This phrase is not a scripture verse but a logical conclusion from such passages as Luke 10:19. "Behold, I give you the authority to trample on serpents and scorpions, and over all the power of the enemy, and nothing shall by any means hurt you"; James 4:7, "Resist the devil and he will flee from you"; and Ephesians 6:12, "For we do not wrestle against flesh and blood, but against principalities, against powers, against the rulers of the darkness of this age, against spiritual hosts of wickedness in the heavenly places."

Positive: It is foolish to ignore the devil's involvement in our lives. The Bible is clear that there are forces of darkness that are seeking to oppose the advancement of God's kingdom in us and our geographical locations. We must become aware of the tactics of our enemy and learn how to walk in victory over him.

We will have a crack in our spiritual foundation if we think that spiritual warfare is primarily "beating up on the devil." Jesus already did this on the cross. Our main warfare is battling our own thoughts rather than fighting Satan. (This truth is supported by the great spiritual warfare passage in 2 Corinthians 10:4-5.) "For the weapons of our warfare are not carnal but mighty in God for pulling down strongholds, casting down arguments and every high thing that exalts itself against the knowledge of God, bringing every thought into captivity to the obedience of Christ." The only instruction that is given for how to "pull down strongholds" is the "capturing" of every lying thought that we might think.

Conclusion: The anointing of God (through people) can break the "yoke" of Satan's hold on lives. This freedom will not last if our thoughts remain in agreement with Satan's lies (even after a powerful encounter with the Holy Spirit). The real battle is in our minds. As we renew our minds concerning Satan's defeat and replace his lies with truth, we will walk in increasing freedom over the devil and bring freedom to others.

#23 *The Lord gives and the Lord takes away*

Context: In Job chapter 1, Job lost most of his family due to disaster, and his health was also in a crisis. In response to this he said: "Naked I came from my mother's womb, And naked shall I return there. The LORD gave, and the LORD has taken away; Blessed be the name of the LORD" (Job 1:21-22).

Positive: Job is an example to us of worshiping and trusting God in the toughest of times (just like Paul and Silas did in Acts 16:25).

There will be a crack in our spiritual foundation if we believe that God can, and sometimes will, take away our family, our health, our finances, and our possessions as part of His plan for our lives. This crack will exist whether we believe that God directly takes these things or if we believe He "allows" the devil to take them. Either of these belief systems will result in a double mindedness in prayer and faith. In addition to this, Job's conclusion that "the Lord takes away" was an analysis that is inconsistent with basic spiritual laws as set forth in scripture. When God said to Satan in Job 1:12, "Behold, all that he has is in your power", He was more likely stating a reality that already existed (because of Job's fear – see Job 3:25), and not a granting of permission to attack Job. Any other conclusion would lead to hopelessness, prayerlessness and fatalism.

Conclusion: We know God inspired all of Scripture, but not every quote of people in the Bible is God's thoughts* (consider Solomon's words in Ecclesiastes). Job's attitude of loving and blessing God during the hardest of times is powerful and is a model for us. We should not however allow Job's experience and conclusions to create our beliefs concerning the reason for negative things in life. If we accept a theology that "the Lord gives and the Lord takes away" in the areas of our health, protection and loved ones; then there can be little faith in prayer. This would not be in harmony with the life of Jesus and the message of the New Testament.

* We cannot develop our doctrine on a subject from one or two passages, but we need to study the entire Bible on that issue (with special emphasis on the New Testament).

#24 *God will do it in His time*

Context: Ecclesiastes 3:1-8 speaks concerning this, "To everything there is a season, <u>A time for every purpose under heaven</u>: A time to be born, And a time to die; A time to plant, And a time to pluck what is planted; A time to kill, And a time to heal; A time to break down, And a time to build up; A time to weep, And a time to laugh; A time to mourn, And a time to dance . . . " I Peter 5:6,7 adds, "Therefore humble yourselves under the mighty hand of God, that He may exalt you <u>in due time,</u> casting all your care upon Him, for He cares for you."

Positive: God's timing is important for us to understand. The principle of <u>seed time and harvest</u> reveals there is a time to plant a seed by faith in every aspect of our lives, and then we wait by faith (without anxious care) for our "due time" to experience its harvest. Also, concerning God's timing, we realize He moves people and events to a <u>perfect timing</u> in response to prayer and faith.

There will be a crack in our spiritual foundation if we believe that God has a blueprint plan that He is implementing which has nothing to do with the actions, prayers and beliefs of people. It is important to acknowledge that our choices and beliefs can speed up, slow down or stop God's "will." (Consider what happened in Jesus' home town in Mark 6.) 2 Peter 3:11-12 speaks of this concerning the last days, ". . . since all these things will be dissolved, what manner of persons ought you to be in holy conduct and godliness, looking for and <u>hastening the coming</u> <u>of the day</u> of God." It is amazing to know that we can influence the timing of Christ's return - just as Jesus' mother "sped up" the time of when her Son was going to start doing miracles (see John 2).

Conclusion: Doing the right thing at the wrong time is a problem, just as it is foolish to ignore God's timing in our lives and circumstances. It is also silly to sit back and wait for God to do what He has commissioned us to get done. God's timing truly has a lot to do with us. It is important to realize that His "will" is more about our involvement in an event, than a specific "something" to happen at a certain time.

#25 *The greatest among you will be your servant*

Context: "But he who is greatest among you shall be your servant. And whoever exalts himself will be humbled, and he who humbles himself will be exalted" (Matthew 23:11-12). "Whoever wishes to be great among you must be your servant, and whoever wishes to be first among you must be your slave; just as the Son of Man came not to be served but to serve . . . ." (Matthew 20:26-28).

Positive: Everyone must have a servant's heart. No Christian should ever come to the place where he or she is too "spiritual" to be a servant. We are not only to serve in practical, helpful ways; but we also need to recognize that we are to give our lives fully to Christ to serve people's need of salvation, deliverance, healing, provision, family restoration and the finding of life's purpose.

There will be a crack in our spiritual foundation if we believe that servanthood means that we are only to wait for God's commands before we think, dream or act. Remember, Jesus said in John 15:15, "No longer do I call you servants . . . but I have called you friends . . ." David was a friend of God, and he wanted to build a temple for his Friend. God said, "I chose David to be over My people Israel. Now it was in the heart of my father David to build a temple for the name of the LORD God of Israel. But the LORD said to my father David, 'Whereas it was in your heart to build a temple for My name, you did well that it was in your heart'" (I Kings 8:16-18). There was a co-laboring between a dedicated person and God.

Conclusion: Psalm 37:4 says, "Delight yourself also in the LORD, And He shall give you the desires of your heart." It is necessary to be a servant, but it is also vital to know that God does not intend for us to be spiritual robots. We are to increasingly trust our ideas and instincts as we live out John 15:7. "If you abide in Me, and My words abide in you, you will ask what you desire, and it shall be done for you."

#26 *All Christians must go through a personal wilderness or desert experience*

Context: Many biblical characters faced a wilderness experience of difficulty before they realized their destiny. Moses, David, Abraham, Jacob, Joseph and others went through a time of breaking of their self-will and a seeming death of their dreams concerning the future. Some spent a lengthy time in a literal desert. Many today teach that we too must go through similar times.

Positive: The children of Israel had to kill giants that were blocking their Promised Land. They were to move through the wilderness to battle and defeat these "lying beings" that were standing between them and their inheritance. Each of us must take the truth that we hear on spiritual mountaintops and move through a "valley" (a wilderness of contrary looking circumstances) where we defeat giants of old thought patterns that have kept us intimidated and defeated. These desert-type happenings can teach us to trust God, to release personal agendas, to have pride reduced from our lives and to move us from formula Christianity to having a deep and intimate relationship with our God.

There will be a crack in our spiritual foundation if we think that the wilderness is difficulty sent by God to break us; instead of it being "a swimming upstream" with God's promises against old thought "currents." Those who believe that negative circumstances are what break us (and make us usable) will actually attract this kind of experience. God did not call the Children of Israel to spend forty years in the wilderness. Their unbelief and word curses kept them there. Many Christians today are stuck in a similar happening and mistakenly think it is God's will. Remember, Jesus only spent 40 days in the wilderness. He came out by resisting the enemy through the inspired truth that was "hid in His heart" (see Matt 4).

Conclusion: Everyone needs to find God personally. We cannot ride continually on the victories of others. We must learn how to have personal victory in tough and dry circumstances. With that said, we also need to know that the length of our stay in the desert is largely up to us. Will it be forty years or will we, like Jesus, use the Word and find the way to get out of the wilderness?

#27 *You did not have enough faith to be healed*

Context: "Now He (Jesus) could do no mighty work there (in his home town), except that He laid His hands on a few sick people and healed them. And He marveled because of their unbelief. Then He went about the villages in a circuit, teaching" (Mark 6:5,6).

Positive: I John 5:4 gives us a key to walking in victory (which includes our health). "For whatever is born of God overcomes the world. And this is the victory that has overcome the world—our faith." It would be foolish to discount the role of faith concerning the advancement of God's kingdom promises in our lives. Jesus frequently spoke of the power of faith in seeing healing and wholeness manifest. One classic passage is in Mark 9 where a father implores Jesus to help his son saying " '. . . but if You can do anything, have compassion on us and help us.' Jesus said to him, 'If you can believe, all things are possible to him who believes.'" The man understood what Jesus said and immediately cried out and said with tears, "Lord, I believe; help my unbelief!"

There will be a crack in our spiritual foundation if we overemphasize the role of personal faith and underemphasize additional important factors concerning healing such as: 1) <u>Corporate faith</u> – Jesus called the disciples in Mark 9 a faithless <u>generation</u> when they were unable to help the man's son. He did not rebuke the boy or the father, but he did chastise the disciples for the lack of healing/deliverance. 2) <u>Other spiritual laws</u> that need to be addressed besides faith – such as forgiveness, eliminating self-imposed word curses, etc. 3) <u>The need for perseverance</u> – those believing for healing for themselves and others need to contend for its manifestation without complicating matters further by making concluding statements about there being a lack of faith.

Conclusion: Faith is vital and important for healing. We must though make a greater emphasis of celebrating faith's growth rather than focusing on its apparent lack in lives.

#28 *We are living in the last days*

Context: Matthew 24:42-44 is a passage that points us to a last days attitude. "Watch therefore, for you do not know what hour your Lord is coming. But know this, that if the master of the house had known what hour the thief would come, he would have watched and not allowed his house to be broken into. Therefore you also be ready, for the Son of Man is coming at an hour you do not expect."

Positive: Just as a person close to death is much more likely to concentrate on what is really important in life, there can be powerful motivation toward urgency and godly focus if we think that we have a limited amount of days left.

There will be a crack in our spiritual foundation if we allow a last day's emphasis to create fatalism in us about the future. This crack will grow wider if we unconsciously expect things to get worse around us in the end times (for our lives, our families, our communities, our nation and for the world). We will find that we are unable to believe God for revival in the nations of the world. Instead of believing and tenaciously claiming Psalms 2:8 for the people of the world ("Ask of me and I will give you the nations for your inheritance"), we will have uncertainty in our intercession. If the enemy can reduce our expectation of seeing people powerfully touched by Jesus (because, after all, it is the end times), then we have been duped into becoming spectators instead of world changing participants in life.

Conclusion: In describing the events of the day of Pentecost, Peter says, "But this is what was spoken by the prophet Joel: 'And it shall come to pass in the last days', says God, 'That I will pour out of My Spirit on all flesh . . .' " (Acts 2:17,18). Peter quotes Joel who said the events of Acts 2 were end time events. We would do well to model our end time behavior and attitudes after the book of Acts (for they were in the last days too), not after those who would embrace a defensive or spectator mentality.

#29 *God won't override someone's free will*

Context: "The Lord is not slack concerning His promise, as some count slackness, but is long-suffering toward us, not willing that any should perish but that all should come to repentance" (I Peter 3:9). God's heart is for every person to be in a right relationship with Him, but He waits for them to make that decision (and does not force them to do so).

Positive: As the verse above indicates, God is long-suffering (patient) toward us. He is a "whosoever God" who gives every person the free choice to choose Him or to not to choose Him. "For God so loved the world that He gave His only begotten Son, that whoever believes in Him should not perish but have everlasting life" (John 3:16). Even though God desires to influence every person toward repentance through the prayers, faith and obedience of His people; He has not created robots that are predestined to be one way or another.

There will be a crack in our foundation if we believe that we are not capable of bringing a tremendous and powerful influence on people (which will make it very difficult for them to reject God's plan for their lives). The power of prayer, faith, love, fasting, prophecy, wisdom, impartation, "speaking life", and standing on the promises of God are mighty weapons that can free those who have been blinded by Satan (2 Corinthians 4:4). Once the blinders have been removed and God is seen as He really is, it would be a hard thing indeed for a person to reject our Savior. Yes, this person's "free will" has not been "overridden", but it has been influenced greatly in the right direction.

Conclusion: Does a dog have a free will if a piece of steak is placed in front of his nose? In one sense the answer is "yes"; but in a greater sense, the answer is a definite "No!" In the same way we have the awesome privilege of putting the true Jesus in front of people. We must be diligent in using our spiritual weapons for others and not become passive because of a "God does not override a person's free will" belief system. Let us never doubt that we have the spiritual arsenal necessary to radically influence people towards making their decision for Jesus Christ and His will.

#30 *All who desire to live godly in Christ Jesus will suffer persecution*

Context: "But you (Timothy) have carefully followed my doctrine, manner of life, purpose, faith, long-suffering, love, perseverance, persecutions, afflictions, which happened to me at Antioch, at Iconium, at Lystra—what persecutions I endured. And out of them all the Lord delivered me. Yes, and all who desire to live godly in Christ Jesus will suffer persecution" (2 Timothy 3:10-12).

Positive: All Christians need to have a willingness to be mistreated (and even die if necessary) for their faith in Jesus. Those who are on the front lines of bringing Christ to godless and demonically ruled cultures can especially face challenging situations. Paul is an example of this, even though he was delivered out of all of them.

There will be a crack in our spiritual foundation if we believe that we will be disliked because we're a Christian. It is unwise to believe that non-Christians (or even church people) will reject us. It is better to believe that the force of favor will cause prospering in all situations, even in godless places (such as what happened with Daniel and Joseph in the Old Testament). Favor will cause people to have a desire to cooperate with us. To increase favor I Timothy 2:1-3 exhorts us to pray so " . . . that we may lead a quiet and peaceable life in all godliness and reverence. For this is good and acceptable in the sight of God our Savior." Remember that Jesus "increased . . . in favor with God and men" (Luke 2:52). Even though Christ's end purpose was a sacrificial death for us, we realize that increasing favor was a key to His life (and so it is to be with us).

Concluding Thoughts: Martyrdom and mistreatment are a reality for Christians, especially in places that are long-standing strongholds of the devil. With that said, it is unwise for us to expect a life of rejection from people. Often our "persecution" is the result of poor people skills, a lack of wisdom or a lack of prayer (consider James' death and Peter's deliverance in Acts 12). In addition to this, it is important to understand that the expectation of favor or the expectation of "persecution" can attract either to our lives. We would do well to anticipate the force of favor to open many doors to us for the kingdom's sake. Others will be glad we did.

#31 *The anointing of God sets people free*

Context: Jesus said in John 20:21, "As the Father has sent Me, so I send you." In Luke 4:18 Jesus describes how the Father sent Him: "The Spirit of the Lord is upon Me because He has anointed Me to preach the gospel to the poor; He has sent me to heal the brokenhearted, to proclaim liberty to the captives and recovery of sight to the blind, to set at liberty those who are oppressed." Acts 10:38 reinforces this, "How God anointed Jesus . . . with the Holy Spirit and with power, who went about doing good and healing all who were oppressed by the devil, for God was with Him."

Positive: Jesus claimed that the anointing of the Spirit on His life was the key to setting people free from bondage, emotional difficulties, spiritual blindness and poverty. When He was baptized in the Spirit, He became anointed to do what He could not do in the first thirty years of His life. We too are called to receive by faith an infusion of power (an anointing) to "set people free." We must believe that one encounter with the anointing of God can change a life forever.

There will be a crack in our spiritual foundation if we believe that the devil is primarily resisted and defeated by a spirit encounter instead of a truth revelation. The power of God does set people wonderfully free, but staying free comes from believing truth instead of lies. In the long run, it isn't the beliefs of the one praying for us that matters most, but it is our own beliefs that will set the course of our lives. Jesus defeated the devil in the wilderness by speaking the truth that He believed (see Matthew 4:1-11). Our Lord powerfully reinforced this in John 8:31-32, "If you abide in My word, you are My disciples indeed; and you will know the truth and the truth will set you free."

Conclusion: Oh how we need a greater demonstration of the anointing of God in our lives and our ministries. We must pursue its manifestation with bulldog tenacity. We must though avoid the tendency to depend on the anointing of "super Christians" and special meetings to make us free (instead of knowing the truth about God, our circumstances, our past, our future and our identity in Christ).

#32 *No man can control the tongue*

Context: "For every kind of beast and bird, of reptile and creature of the sea, is tamed and has been tamed by mankind. But no man can tame the tongue. It is an unruly evil, full of deadly poison. With it we bless our God and Father, and with it we curse men who have been made in the similitude of God" (James 3:7-9).

Positive: It has been said that if we talk long enough, we will say something wrong. It is the nature of people who are disconnected from God to gravitate toward poor and sinful choices, and this certainly includes saying destructive words in the form of gossip, cussing, angry outbursts, criticism, self-pronounced curses, lying, slander, and general negativity.

There will be a crack in our spiritual foundation if we think that we are destined to (and should expect) negative speech in our lives, in our families and in our churches. Instead, we need to see hope in verses such as Ephesians 4:29, "Let no corrupt words proceed out your mouth . . . " (because we understand that we will never be commanded to do something we cannot do). This truth goes far beyond stopping the negative talk; but, more importantly, it teaches us the powerful principle of speaking life as a positive force in all aspects of life. Truly "the power of life and death is in the tongue, and those who love it will eat the fruit of it" (Proverbs 18:21). Those who love it are those who proactively, enthusiastically and joyfully use words to plant seeds for the future. (They "plant" words that will bring great fruit to "eat" in relationships, health, ministry, evangelism, kingdom advancement, vocation, finances, protection and overall blessing.)

Conclusion: We must be vigilant to put a guard over our mouths so that we don't curse others or ourselves, but there is a higher goal than this. Truly, our tongues can be controlled if we allow the Holy Spirit to empower and "visionate" us to the point where we declare with passion, "I love it! I have another opportunity today through my words to impart grace to others, to sow abundant life into my (and my family's) future and to speak of the wonderful works of God.

#33 *We don't need to be part of a church to be a Christian*

Context: This is a phrase that is said often. In our discussion here, we are referring to the church as a place where people gather weekly (or more) to worship God together and to spend time with like-minded people.

Positive: It's true that we receive eternal life through faith in Christ, not by attending or joining a church. As individuals, we are able to have wonderful fellowship and experiences with God through personal prayer, Bible reading, ministering to and helping others, and through various contact with other Christians.

There will be a crack in our spiritual foundation if we undervalue the role the church has in our lives and in God's plan. Here's five reasons the church is important: 1) it provides positive peer pressure to live victoriously (I John 1:7) through a regular connection with people who honor God and the Bible; 2) it allows us to use our God given gifts while being joined with other parts of the "body of Christ" as described in I Corinthians 12 and Ephesians 4:15-16; 3) we can be equipped and trained by anointed leadership for our purpose in life (Ephesians 4:11-16); 4) the committed relationships in a church cause us to "grow up" and become consistent in our Christianity - just as marriage and other family covenants cause us to mature; and 5) church provides an exponential increase of our potential to change the world when we join others with our talents, prayers, faith, finances, and fulfilling our Great Commission (Matthew 28:18-20) of reaching the world for Christ.

Conclusion: There may be situations where we're unable to find a local church to be involved with, and there may be seasons of our lives where our participation is less because of specific things happening in us; but we must be careful of trying to live apart from a consistent connection to God's people. Successful living requires a clear order of personal priorities. God needs to be #1 and it is clear from scripture (and from life experience) that if we don't consistently give him the first part of our day in prayer and the Word, and the first part of our week in worship and fellowship, we will have difficulty truly living for God.

#34 *It's not about me*

Context: "Let nothing be done through selfish ambition or conceit, but in lowliness of mind let each esteem others better than himself. Let each of you look out not only for his own interests, but also for the interests of others. Let this mind be in you which was also in Christ Jesus, who . . . made Himself of no reputation, taking the form of a bondservant . . . " (Philippians 2:3-7).

Positive: Jesus has a way of delivering us from selfishness and self-centeredness. He calls us to get our eyes off of ourselves, and put our sight on Him and the needs of other people. He has delivered us from self-pity, self-preservation, self-promotion, self-protection, self-reliance, self-righteousness and self-justifying behavior; and He has made a way for us to stay free from them. We hopefully have learned (like a young child) that the world does not revolve around us. (If not, we will be constantly depressed, frustrated, angry, and have difficulty in relationships.)

We will have a crack in our spiritual foundation if, in our zeal to be selfless, we don't have a clear plan to stay healthy physically, emotionally, spiritually, financially, mentally and relationally. What good is it if we help people now, but experience burnout early in life because we failed to understand our priorities and didn't follow basic wisdom for successful living. Also, those who are constantly taking care of the "needs" of others are often enabling those people to be increasingly irresponsible and dependent on them. Finally, it is necessary to guard against using our zealous serving and "selfless Christianity" as an escape or justification for why we don't get help in our own lives for major unresolved personal issues and/or family dysfunction.

Conclusion: It is truly "not about me." As Jesus did, I must "lay my life down" for others. We do though need to understand that this self-sacrifice is not always about meeting the immediate needs and wants of others (because "laying our lives down" is also a commitment to <u>personal increase</u> so we can meet multiplied more needs and to prepare ourselves to be able to give much more in the future).

#35 *Let all things be done decently and in order*

Context: In I Corinthians 14, Paul explains the purpose of prophecy and tongues (and gives guidelines for their use). In concluding his teaching, he writes, "Therefore, brethren, desire earnestly to prophesy, and do not forbid to speak with tongues. <u>Let all things be done decently and in order</u>" (I Cor. 14:40).

Positive: The Corinthian church seemed to be a "free for all" in the use (or abuse) of spiritual gifts. Apparently their meetings were dominated with lengthy messages in tongues. In his letter to them, Paul painstakingly gives direction and "order" for the proper use of tongues and spiritual gifts. He strongly encourages their use, but provides boundaries and the spiritual reasons for their operation. Church leaders today also need to guide the use of spiritual gifts so that things are done decently and in order so that true edification will occur.

There will be a crack in our spiritual foundation if we think that "decent and in order" means that nothing odd or discomforting will happen in our church meetings. We need to realize that wherever there is new life, there will be "messes"; and wherever there is true spiritual fire, there will be some "wild fire" happening that seems out of control. Cemeteries are decent and in order, but there is no life there. Many churches are so decent and in order that encounters with God are rare or non-existent.

Conclusion: We need to pray for church leaders as they seek to lead with wisdom concerning the "move" of the Holy Spirit. On the one hand, they must establish order, structure and boundaries concerning the operation and manifestation of the Spirit in meetings. On the other hand, leaders need to create a "wineskin" of freedom to experience God powerfully and spontaneously in ways that some would say is not decent and in order. This wineskin is made up of "ingredients" that: 1) encourages Christ-centered risk taking, 2) trains in the gifts of the Spirit, 3) empowers and trusts people to minister in the "anointing", 4) has strong accountability, 5) values joy, 6) does not over-plan meetings, and 7) esteems passionate worship. This wineskin may not bring about "safe predictability", but the results will be "decent and in order" in God's eyes.

#36 *God helps those who help themselves*

Context: This phrase is an ancient proverb that appears in the literature of many cultures, including a 1736 edition of Benjamin Franklin's Poor Richard's Almanac. It does not however appear in the Bible.

Positive: The Bible has many promises that depend on us doing our part for them to be realized. Some examples are as follows: 1) if we draw near to Him, He will draw near to us (James 4:8); 2) if we call on His name, we will be saved (Romans 10:13); 3) if we sow to the Spirit, we will reap life (Galatians 6:8); 4) if we pray, He will answer (Matthew 7:7); 5) if we forgive, we will be forgiven (Matthew 6:14); and 6) if we give, He will give back to us (Luke 6:38). Indeed, there are many ways that God seemingly "helps" those who are seeking Him, loving Him, honoring His spiritual laws and are devoted to serving Him.

There will be a crack in our spiritual foundation if we believe that God is more concerned with what we do than what we believe. Certainly good works are important, but they are not what saves us or what primarily moves the hand of God in our lives. Consider Ephesians 2:8-9 – "For by grace you have been saved through faith, and that not of yourselves; it is the gift of God, not of works, lest anyone should boast." Galatians 3:2-5 takes this further - "This only I want to learn from you: Did you receive the Spirit by the works of the law, or by the hearing of faith? Are you so foolish? Having begun in the Spirit, are you now being made perfect by the flesh? . . . Therefore He who supplies the Spirit to you and works miracles among you, does He do it by the works of the law, or by the hearing of faith?" It is obvious that God ultimately "helps" those who believe and have faith, not those who think their moral superiority (works of the law) attracts God's blessing. Truly, Christ came because we ultimately could not help ourselves.

Conclusion: Hard work is a great quality, but God is not looking to "help those who help themselves." He is looking for those who will have a radical belief in His Son and in His Word (the Bible), which will release a supernatural, divine empowerment that "helps" them do what they never thought they could do.

#37 *Sincerity and having a good heart are the most important things in the Christian life*

Context: We are instructed in many places in the Bible to be pure in heart, to be sincere and to have good motives in what we do.

Positive: Two definitions for sincere are: 1) honest and unaffected in a way that shows what is said is really meant; and 2) based on what is truly and deeply felt (Encarta® World English Dictionary). These are qualities that are essential for being an effective Christian. In addition to this, the word "good" means to "have or show an upright and virtuous character." These qualities are vital for our lives. It is absolutely necessary that we "go after" having a good heart which possesses patience, kindness, loyalty, honesty, genuine care for others, and which esteems integrity & honor in relationships over our desire for personal gain, money or position in life.

There will be a crack in our spiritual foundation if we believe that "being sincere" and "nice" overrides negative beliefs and poor personal priorities. There are many sincere people who are sincerely wrong. There are numerous Christians who have good hearts, but still are imprisoned in a "wilderness Christianity". John the Baptist and Jesus did not say, "Be sincere, for the kingdom of God is at hand!" No, they said, "Repent, for the kingdom of God is at hand." Repentance is changing the way we think so that we believe God's promises instead of lies. Unless we continually renew our minds (Romans 12:2), we will not have lasting breakthrough, even if we have a good heart. Repentance also involves doing things God's way and not our own way. Wrong choices, even with a good heart, can cause great problems.

Conclusion: Every Christian needs to strive to have a sincere heart and good motives in all that is done. Without this, we are headed for a shipwreck in our future. Even so, we also need to recognize that these great qualities are not enough to defeat the devil in our lives or see the kingdom advance through us. Therefore, let us also pursue increasing revelation of God and His Word.

#38 *People close to God are misunderstood and struggle in relationships with people*

Context: This is not a Bible verse, but is the belief and experience of some.

Positive: Those who "shut themselves in with God" can seem "out of step" with what is going on in the lives of others. These people will have higher standards in decision-making and in lifestyle choices. This can be uncomfortable and convicting for non-believers and half-hearted Christians. Church attendees who are less serious about their faith will sometimes criticize passionate saints for being fanatical and "too heavenly minded to be any earthly good."

There will be a crack in our spiritual foundation if we believe that continued strained relationships are a sign of our "closeness" to God (or a sign that people are rejecting something righteous in us). "People problems" are often an indication of immaturity or the need of healing from past relationship wounds. Consider this: If we are only respected and liked by those who have spent <u>little time</u> with us (and don't know us well), then we have a <u>character problem</u>. Too often, misunderstandings and problems in relationships come from undervaluing I Corinthians 13 relational love. "Spirituality" that exists without agape love is often shown by being ungrateful, frequently irritable, undependable, tactless in speech, rude, "using people", poor in listening, grumbling & complaining about others, dishonoring & hurtful to immediate family members, and irresponsible for past relationship "messes" that need to be "cleaned up."

Conclusion: We don't want to compromise our convictions to be acceptable to lukewarm Christians and non-believers, but we certainly don't want to see rejection as a "badge of honor" to prove we are close to God. We must be careful that we don't justify relationship breakdowns, and then focus on the faults of those seemingly against us. It is the wise person who gets to the root of his or her "people problem issues" so that there can be true respect from family members, close associates, and others. Realize this: everyone may not like us; but if people don't respect us, we have work to do to clean up our past relationship "messes."

#39 *And every branch that bears fruit He prunes*

Context: "I am the true vine, and My Father is the vinedresser. Every branch in Me that does not bear fruit He takes away; and every branch that bears fruit He prunes, that it may bear more fruit. You are already clean because of the word which I have spoken to you. Abide in Me, and I in you. As the branch cannot bear fruit of itself, unless it abides in the vine, neither can you, unless you abide in Me" (John 15:1-4).

Positive: Plants need to be pruned for a variety of reasons. Pruning allows them to be shaped to desirable sizes and characteristics to compliment the rest of a garden or yard. Also, pruning removes dead, diseased or damaged branches or stems. This increases the overall well-being and beauty of our vegetation. God also prunes our lives of old thought patterns and old behaviors that (if not pruned) will hinder us from bearing greater fruit in the days ahead.

We will have a crack in our spiritual foundation if we believe that God prunes us primarily through negative circumstances, rather than by "cutting back" old belief patterns in our lives. It is not our actions that is our biggest problem, but it is the way we think. It is difficult or impossible to go to a higher level in obedience or in our circumstances without first going to a higher level in what we believe. The main reason we are not bearing more fruit now is because there are still strongholds of "dead beliefs" that must be pruned back so we can bear more fruit.

Conclusion: God is pruning each of us for a higher purpose. There may be difficult circumstances involved in this process, but the goal is something much higher than just strengthening our character or growing in perseverance. Our "heavenly gardener" is ready to "snip" off the lies we have believed that have restricted our lives. Let's help Him do it by "declaring war" once more on our real enemy: the falsehoods in our thinking that rob us of faith, hope and love.

#40 *God is going to kill you*

The Context: This phrase is not in the Bible, but is sometimes used in messages and books to describe the dying to self-will that must happen in a Christian's life. It is presented often like this: "We ask Jesus in our hearts; and we expect to be blessed, but we find out that God really wants to kill us."

The Positive: We cannot simply add Jesus to our own plans, priorities and ways of doing things. We have to "die" to "doing our own thing." Our old responses and thinking patterns are to be put on "death row." All of this can be somewhat surprising (and at times painful) because we underestimated the addiction we had to our old ways. Like a drug addict who is going "cold turkey", we can experience withdrawals (from our old thinking patterns) that seem to be "killing us." This experience happens to some degree every time we move forward in Christ.

We will have a crack in our foundation if we believe that God desires to bring us into constant hard times to mature us. This doctrinal belief will actually be a magnet for more difficulty. Those who think that God makes our lives miserable to help us grow would need to report Him to the authorities for child abuse. Also, God does not want to "kill" our uniqueness and creativity. We are not to be robots and clones of one another, but are to live uniquely in our personality and calling.

Concluding Thoughts: Religion presents God as the great, cosmic "killjoy." We must be careful that we don't reinforce this false concept by overemphasizing dying to self (and underemphasizing the lifestyle of a resurrected, empowered life). It's true that we have a war going on in us, but that war is primarily won by "hiding God's Word in our hearts that we might not sin against Him" (Psalm 119:11) and by "walking in the Spirit" (focusing on the positive) so that we "will not fulfill the lusts of the flesh" (Galatians 5:16).

#41 *Partial obedience is not obedience*

The Context: This phrase is not a Bible verse, but it is illustrated in I Samuel 15 where King Saul did not fully obey the command by Samuel concerning the Amalakites and King Agag. Saul was sharply rebuked for this and ultimately lost his kingdom because of being double-minded and half-hearted in obedience.

The Positive: It is vital for Christians to follow through on the Word of the Lord. It can be easy to start something, and then not finish or do so in an incomplete manner. In the Parable of the Sower (Mark 4), the second seed gives insight on this. That seed fell on shallow ground that represents those who lose interest when the "excitement" wears off. This shallowness of commitment and follow-through is a huge issue for us and is to be resisted just as much as any other sin. We must build the internal "muscle" of finishing what we start. David "finished Goliath off" by cutting his head off. We too are to go against our feelings and do what God has said (and what we have said we would do).

There will be a crack in our Christian foundation if we believe that only "successful obedience" is true obedience. Just as a baby learns to walk, we too must learn how to obey God in many areas of our lives. When we seem to fail in attempting to live at a higher level of Christianity, we need to realize that "falling down" often precedes "walking" consistently.

Concluding Thoughts: Learning to follow through on what God has spoken to us is important. It is also vital to understand that as we grow in God we will make mistakes as we are learning to truly follow the Lord's leading. (Remember Peter, who stepped out of the boat onto the water with his eyes on Jesus, but began to sink when he took his eyes off of his Savior?) Like Peter, those who seek to obey what the Lord is saying will appear to fail more than those who are "playing it safe" from inside of the boat. Let's not become condemned when we seemingly fail as we step out of the boat of past comforts and ways of doing things. And, more importantly, let's not revert back to a comfortable and "failure-proof" Christianity that settles for mediocrity and non-accountability for what God has told us to do.

#42 *Calling those things which do not exist as though they did*

The Context: "As it is written, 'I have made you a father of many nations', in the presence of Him whom he believed—God, who gives life to the dead and calls those things which do not exist as though they did" (Romans 4:17). In this verse God reveals His strategy for bringing life to dead situations. This method is "naming and calling" things by His promises (instead of what they seem to be). Abram is used as the example of this truth. His miracle manifested after he called himself Abraham (which means "father of a multitude").

The Positive: "Faith comes by hearing and hearing by the Word of God" (Romans 10:17). Our speaking of God's promises not only improves the spiritual atmosphere; but, more importantly, it builds up (edifies) our belief system to truly believe who God says we are and who He says He is. Joel says, "Let the weak say I am strong" (Joel 3:10). "Calling ourselves" by the promises of God is a key for breakthrough in our lives. As long as we "call" ourselves by our past experiences, we are locked into repeating them.

There will be a crack in our spiritual foundation if we think that this verse says the opposite of what it really says. It does not say, "Calling those things that are as though they are not." To do this would be "living in denial." The Bible does not teach us to say, "I am not sick or I am not weak in that area." That would be a lie and a focusing on the negative, rather than concentrating on God's solutions. Some, in the name of faith, have thought that denying the negative is the key to seeing it leave. In reality, the presence of the positive is what evicts the negative. (Remember, the best way to get rid of darkness is to turn on the light!)

Concluding Thoughts: Christians are not to deny the facts of current negative situations. We are called to address these things with responsibility and wisdom. We do however choose to focus more on God's truths and promises rather than just the facts of what is currently happening. As Abraham did, we are called to declare the great, laughable promises over our lives, even when all circumstances are screaming, "It will never happen."

Appendix - Part One - The Promises of God
Antidote to Having Cracks in Our Foundation

2 Peter 1:4 tells us that through God's "exceedingly great and precious promises we participate in the divine nature & escape the corruption that is in the world . . ." Here are seven promises to declare (& believe) that will bring us out of the past & will launch us into God's destiny.

I Have Supernatural Ability – "I can do all things through Christ who strengthens me." Philippians 4:13

I Have Supernatural Hope and Open Doors – "No temptation (trial) has overtaken (me) except such as is common to man, but God is faithful, who will not allow (me) to be tempted beyond what (I am) able, but with the temptation will also make the way of escape, that I may be able to bear it." I Corinthians 10:13

I Have a Supernatural Completion – "I am confident of this very thing, that He who has begun a good work in (me) will complete it until the day of Jesus Christ." Philippians 1:6

I Have Supernatural Answered Prayer – "Now this is the confidence that we have in Him, that if we ask anything according to His will, He hears us. And if we know that He hears us, we know that we have the petitions that we have asked of Him." I John 5:14,15

I Have Supernatural Wisdom – "If any man lacks wisdom, let him ask of God, who gives to all liberally and without reproach, and it will be given to him." James 1:5

I Have Supernatural Provision – ""And (my) God shall supply all (my) need according to His riches in glory by Christ Jesus." Philippians 4:19

I Have Supernatural Assurance – "And we know that all things work together for good to those who love God, to those who are the called according to His purpose." Romans 8:28

I Have a Supernatural Harvest - "He who sows generously reaps generously." 2 Corinthians 9:6. "And let us not grow weary while doing good, for in due season we shall reap if we do not lose heart." Galatians 6:9

Appendix - Part Two
Core Values - Further Repellent to Cracks

The core values below are the core values that Steve and Wendy live by. Add these to the basics of good Christian theology and get ready for increase in your life and ministry.

1. We owe the world an encounter with God therefore we are relentless in the pursuit of His presence and power both inside and outside the church walls (Acts 16:25-34).

2. What we believe after we pray is just as important as what we believe while we pray (Mark 11:24; I John 5:14,15).

3. We see problems as opportunities to see how big our God is (James 1:2-5; Romans 5:3-5).

4. Prayer and worship times (both private and corporate) are foundational to our calling as individuals and as a church (Mark 11:17; John 4:23,24).

5. Celebrating joyously in God's promises and in His goodness (which includes laughing at the lies of the devil) is a secret to our strength (Nehemiah 8:10; Psalms 2:2-4).

6. Training people for ministry, for life skills, and for leadership is central to our fulfilling the great commission (Ephesians 4:11,12; 2 Timothy 2:2).

7. The first step in spiritual warfare is taking every thought captive to the obedience of Christ. Warfare is not beating up on the devil; Jesus already did this. Therefore we proactively capture thoughts that do not glisten with faith, hope and love (2 Corinthians 10:3-5).

8. Personal hope (the confident and optimistic expectation of seeing God's goodness) is to be a major pursuit of our lives. We believe there is hope for every person and every situation we encounter (Romans 5:3,4, I Corinthians 10:13).

9. The power of life and death is in the words that we speak over ourselves, others and every aspect of our lives (Proverbs 18:21).

10. We motivate people through vision, a revelation of God, and the power of God; rather than by guilt, law or condemnation (Proverbs 29:18; Acts 16:30).

11. Honor brings life; therefore we cultivate high levels of respect in all relationships and speak with respect, even if we are in disagreement (Ephesians 6:2,3).

12. The testimony of Jesus is the spirit of prophecy; therefore we place a high value on declaring the great things God has done (Revelation 19:10).

13. Generosity and gratefulness are two gateways for us to experience the promises of God in our lives and in our church (Acts 10:2,3; Psalms 100:4).

14. We pursue relationship with spiritual fathers and mothers and desire them to speak into our lives (Acts 16:13-15).

15. We understand that to walk in wisdom we must have a plan for our personal and ministry growth (I Timothy 4:14-16).

16. As new covenant believers, we repent primarily to God's promises and our prophetic destiny rather than just from our sins and weaknesses. We are more for good than we are against evil (2 Corinthians 3:7-18).

17. We create a culture where failure is a learning experience, not an identity, as we seek to walk in higher levels in Christ (Philippians 3:12-14).

18. We are called to empower and support other churches/ministries and their leaders (Colossians 4:12-13).

19. We believe that those we are ministering to want to serve God and that they will rise to our belief in them (1 Corinthians 13:7).

20. Healthy ministry to the church and world must result from a greater emphasis on being healthy in our immediate family relationships - especially our marriages (1 Timothy 3:2,4-5).

21. Integrity, being an example of Christian living, and having a good reputation are foundational for effective ministry and leadership (1 Timothy 3:1-5).

22. God has delegated His authority to us to enforce Christ's victory over demons, sickness and lack. Therefore, like Jesus and the apostles, we speak to mountains, to situations, and to sickness & disease (Mark 11:22-24; James 4:7).

23. All that we do must have a "I Corinthians 13 love" as its foundation or else it is worthless (1 Corinthians 3:1-5; and chapter 13).

24. The quality of our lives is based on the quality of our commitments. We make covenant commitments to God, to family, to a local church, and to a core group of people in our lives (Ephesians chapters 4:1 - 6:9).

25. Servanthood is essential to greatness in God's kingdom. Therefore, we strive to cultivate and demonstrate a true servant's heart in the church and in the world (Matthew 20:24-28).

26. Because God's kingdom is proactive, we don't wait for things to happen, but we seek out opportunities for light to shine in darkness – being empowered by God's love, sensitivity and wisdom (Matthew 10:5-8).

Appendix Three
Three Teachings from *Igniting Faith in 40 Days*
A Powerful Devotional Book
by Steve and Wendy Backlund

#1
A Lying Apple Tree?
***Calling those things that are not . . .* (Rom 4:17)**

An apple tree will produce apples because of what it is. When it is young, it will have no apples; but it still must say, "I am an apple tree." When it is winter and there are no leaves or apples; it still says, "I am an apple tree." Is it lying at those times? No. It would be lying to say anything different.

Many Christians have a hard time saying who God says they are when no fruit is manifesting in that particular area. Could they be "too young" in that truth to be fruitful? Could they be in a season where that dimension of the Christian life is being pruned back for future growth? Either way, it does not mean they are lying when they say, "I am anointed, prosperous, delivered, healed, righteous, strong etc."

Joel 3:10 says, "Let the weak say I am strong." We don't deny the fact of weakness, but we focus on the greater truth that we are strong in Him.

Again, because the Word says we ARE these things, we would be untruthful to say anything different. Let's not lie against the truth. Indeed we ARE what the Bible says we are.

Declare: I am who the Word says I am. I have a sound mind. I have great favor with God and man. People love me. I am a happy person. I love life and enjoy every day. I am healed. I have abundant provision. I am blessed and protected. I increasingly know who and what I am in Christ. I make a tremendous difference for Christ wherever I go.

Exerpt from Igniting Faith in 40 Days
#2

Praying in Faith (Part I)
Mary has chosen the best part **(Luke 10:42)**

Often people spend much effort and time praying over a circumstance hoping that *time and quantity* of prayer will bring the desired result. The hope is that perhaps faith will increase through this effort and thus the prayer will be answered.

This kind of thinking implies that faith is built by the amount of time and energy expended. We need to understand that faith does not come through our effort. Faith is a result of what we "know." Our "measure of faith" (Romans 12:3) will increase in proportion to the revelation we have of God's character, His love, and His promises toward us.

Often we do not realize the value of spending time with God when we are not praying for needs. The reason we worship, quietly wait in His presence, and search the scripture is mainly to build a relationship and to learn about the character, power, and love of God. Our intimacy and relationship with Him will have a direct correlation to our level of faith; not because it "earns" us more authority, but because it gives something for our faith to stand on.

Declare: My trust and faith in God grows in the proportion to how much I know His character, goodness, and trustworthiness. I therefore spend much time in His presence developing intimacy with Him.

Exerpt from *Igniting Faith in 40 Days*
#3

Rose Colored Glasses
. . through . . . Scriptures . . . might have hope (Ro 15:4)

Sometimes optimistic people are accused of seeing life through "rose colored" glasses. Their vision supposedly is affected by an unrealistic perspective that blinds them to life's negatives and accentuates only the positives.

All Christians have predispositions that influence how the Bible is interpreted, and thus how life is viewed. These unconscious inclinations are often influenced by the "traditions of men" which limit positive expectancy for the future (see Mark 7:13).

Romans 15:4 tells us that hope results from proper Bible "learning." Later in verse 13 we are told that joy, peace, and abounding hope come from "believing." There should be a corresponding increase of hope in our lives that is proportional to the amount of the Bible we consume.

Unfortunately, many church teachings limit hope. For example, most "end times" teachings decrease positive expectation for lives, families, cities, and the nations of the world. As a result, many don't live with hope and faith because of a predisposition that believes "the world is getting worse" (and not better). This hopelessness indicates we need an alteration in our interpretation of Scripture. Truly, hope grows with each encounter with God's Word and with the God of hope.

Declare: I see the Bible and life through "blood colored" glasses. I therefore abound in hope for my life and for everyone connected to me. God's promises are true. My prayers are powerful and effective. My hope helps release God's kingdom in our midst.

Appendix Four
Negativity Fast

We urge you to consider going on a fast from negativity for 40 days (or some other length of time). Many cracks in your theological thinking will be addressed as you contnue to pursue God's "higher thoughts" (Isaiah 55:9) on the things in your life. Here are some helpful suggestions on this subject:

What a Negativity Fast is Not:
1. It is not denying that problems exist
2. It is not "stuffing things" that are wrong
3. It is not critical of others who may be struggling
4. It is not irresponsible concerning things that need to be done

What a Negativity Fast Is:
1. It is determining to focus more on God's promises than on problems
2. It is learning to speak with hope about even the toughest of issues
3. It is becoming "solution focused" rather than "problem focused"
4. It is refraining from giving voice to pessimism, self-criticism, criticism of others and other forms of unbelief
5. It is speaking about problems to the right people in the right way
6. It is replacing negative words & thoughts with positive words & thoughts based on the promises of God

Note: It is crucial to not only stop thinking and speaking unbelief and negativity; but to grow in speaking truth, the promises of God, praising God, encouragement to others and thanksgiving. The negative must be replaced with the positive in order for this fast to be effective.

Igniting Faith in 40 Days has been used by many as a daily devotional book to read during a personal or group 40 day negativity fast.